The SACRED ENNEAGRAM WORKBOOK

The SACRED ENNEAGRAM WORKBOOK

CHRISTOPHER L. HEUERTZ

with ESTEE ZANDEE

ZONDERVAN

The Sacred Enneagram Workbook
Copyright © 2019 by Christopher L. Heuertz

Requests for information should be addressed to:
Zondervan, *3900 Sparks Dr. SE, Grand Rapids, Michigan 49546*

ISBN 978-0-310-35846-6 (softcover)

ISBN 978-0-310-35847-3 (ebook)

Author is represented by The Christopher Ferebee Agency, www.christopherferebee.com.

Cover design: Charles Brock | Faceout Studio
Cover illustrations: Shutterstock®
Author photo: Scott Drickey
Interior illustrations: Elnora Turner
Interior design: Kait Lamphere

Printed in the United States of America

19 20 21 22 23 24 25 26 27 28 29 /LSC/ 20 19 18 17 16 15 14 13 12 11 10 9 8 7 6 5 4 3 2 1

Contents

Introduction

Welcome to the journey of discovering your true identity and the spiritual path to becoming the free, unique, and beloved person God created you to be.

In this book, you will learn what the Enneagram is and how it helps us become aware of both our go-to masks and our true essence. This workbook will teach you how to discover your type and show you what your type reveals about your behavior, characteristics, vulnerabilities, and unique giftings. But more than that, you'll explore how the fractals, or patterns, within the Enneagram lead us all into a deeper understanding of who we are, how we can grow, and the unique way each one of us is made to experience the presence of the Divine.

As a companion to *The Sacred Enneagram* by Chris Heuertz, each session of this workbook pairs with a corresponding chapter or chapters. This study was designed to be used either individually or in a group. In each session, you'll find:

- A summary of key concepts from the corresponding chapter of *The Sacred Enneagram*
- Graphs and charts showing the dynamic movements within the Enneagram
- Insightful and inspiring quotes
- Questions to lead you into self-discovery and transformational growth
- Reflection or discussion questions for group use
- A contemplative invitation which will walk you through a mindful practice designed for personal and spiritual wholeness and connection with God

Drawing from decades of in-depth study, mentorships with Mother Teresa and Father Richard Rohr, and years of teaching the Enneagram through contemplative practice, Chris Heuertz offers a profound, life-changing journey into the treasure of your own soul. For anyone ready to move past mere behavior traits and to real, lasting transformation, this book will compassionately guide you through the inner work of finding your way back to your true self and the anchoring presence of a loving God.

FOR PERSONAL USE

As you set out on this path of self-discovery through this workbook, you may like to read the corresponding chapter(s) of *The Sacred Enneagram* first before reflecting on the questions in each session. Alternatively, page numbers are listed throughout so that you can also read *The Sacred Enneagram* side-by-side with this workbook.

You'll find transformational growth through the "Invitations"—step-by-step guides to contemplative practices at the end of each session. To ensure that you have an uninterrupted and meaningful prayer experience, it may be helpful to read through the steps first before starting the exercise.

FOR GROUP USE

It is recommended that the group reads the corresponding chapters of *The Sacred Enneagram* before meeting to discuss the reflection prompts and discussion questions and explore the contemplative practices in this workbook.

The contemplative practices outlined in each session's Invitation are easily practiced in a group setting. Communal silence can be a very meaningful shared experience. However, you may find it helpful for the group facilitator or a volunteer to familiarize themselves with the practice first in order to support the group through each spiritual exercise.

Members of the group may want to mark any questions that they would like the group to focus on prior to meeting—in addition to the group discussion question at the end of each session.

Some of the discussion questions will prompt readers to examine sensitive or even painful memories, so it is important that the group cultivates a space where every participant feels safe—encouraged to open their hearts to others but unpressured to share anything they are not ready to.

A FEW NOTES

Though there are quite a few helpful names for each Enneagram type, this workbook refers to the types by their numbers in an effort to avoid labeling individuals based on their social function rather than the real gift of their true selves.

It is tempting to categorize the people in your life through the lens of the Enneagram. However, it is important to note that typing individuals when they're unsure of their number or before they're ready to fully engage with the Enneagram can be harmful to them and to your relationship. The Enneagram works best when used with grace and compassion, and primarily as a transformational tool between you and God. And so, with such a journey of transformation ahead, let us begin!

> "Dive down into your self and there you will find
> the steps by which you might ascend."
> —*Saint Isaac the Syrian*

All quotes are extracted from *The Sacred Enneagram*
unless otherwise noted.

PART I

FINDING YOURSELF *in the* ENNEAGRAM'S MIRROR

—— 1 ——

The Sacred Enneagram:
Chapters 1 and 2

Exploring Who We Are

Each and every one of us is beautiful and beloved by God. But when it comes to recognizing the truth of our own identities, we all experience a version of blindness that keeps us from seeing ourselves for who we really are. We live unawakened lives marked by lies we tell ourselves about who we think we are—or how we wish to be seen by others. Sadly, most of us do not know that we don't know who we are. We are unaware that we've lost our true self. It often takes an unlikely "other" to remind us what's true: *you are beautiful, you have profound worth, your life is a gift.*

Coming home to our true self sounds great, but it's often hard, monotonous, and sometimes messy work. It is easier to stay hidden, to avoid the hard work of excavating our essence. After all, if you're going to unearth treasure, your hands will get dirty. So as you begin this journey of discovering your true self, it is important to walk this path with compassion.

HOW WE GOT LOST

The contemporary Enneagram of Personality shows us much more than a list of personality traits. It illustrates the nine ways we get lost, but also the nine ways we can come home to our True Self (page 25). It exposes nine ways we lie to ourselves about who we think we are, nine ways we can come clean about those illusions, and nine ways we can find our way back to God.

Tragically, most of us believe that if we build out the mythology of who we think we are, the more attractive our identity will be and the more valuable we become. But when we equate our value with the proofs we collect about our worth—the good (or bad) things we've done, what we have, what others think of us—we create a no-win scenario that always leads to disillusionment and pain because they are just parts, not the whole, of who we are. When we overidentify with our success or failure, we allow these fragments to form the basis of our essence. The inevitable result is that we will fall into an unceasing chase after an unrealistic and unattainable idea of who we think we need to be (page 18). This is how we get ourselves lost. The challenge is to find our way home.

- The fundamental question to the human experience is "Who am I?" (page 16). Our first interaction with a new acquaintance often exposes our fears or insecurities by how we describe ourselves. How do you normally introduce yourself? What do your words and subtext say about what you hold to be most important about your life?

_____

_____

_____

_____

_____

_____

_____

_____

_____

_____

- Exploring the difference between *substance* and *value*, it is suggested that identity answers the question "Who am I?" while dignity answers the question "What am I worth?" (page 17). What does this tell you about your value?

  _____

  _____

  _____

  _____

  _____

- How have you grown estranged from your true self over the years? What thoughts, longings, and emotions come to mind for you when you think about finding the way home to your true self?

  _____

  _____

  _____

  _____

  _____

- Father Richard Rohr gives this warning: *Every unrealistic expectation is a resentment waiting to happen* (page 18). How have you seen this play out in your life?

  _____

  _____

  _____

  _____

  _____

- The three lies that we believe about our identity, as Henri Nouwen famously articulated, are *I am what I have, I am what I do,* and *I am what other people say or think about me* (page 20). How have these lies informed your identity? Which one do you rely on most?

  _____

  _____

  _____

  _____

> "All humanity bears the imprint of the Divine, that we are made in the image of God. This is the starting point for drawing forward our sense of dignity, the intrinsic value that is **ascribed** not **earned**, based on our essence in reflecting a good and loving God."

- Of the three programs for happiness (page 21), which do you gravitate toward: power and control, affection and esteem, or security and survival? How have you experienced the sense of being stuck by overidentifying with these programs?

_____

_____

_____

_____

_____

_____

_____

_____

_____

_____

- The history of the Enneagram (pages 42–51) includes a sad line of broken ties, yet it also includes examples of personal growth and relational reconciliation in the lives of individuals all around the world. How might understanding your identity and the identity of others bring growth and intimacy to your world?

_____

_____

_____

_____

_____

_____

_____

_____

FINDING YOUR TRUE SELF IN THE ENNEAGRAM'S MIRROR

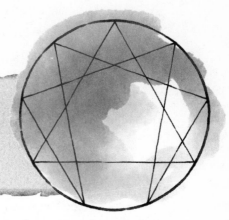

> "This sacred map of the Enneagram is a dynamic and compassionate sketch of possibilities and opportunities which guide us back to our True Self and the anchoring God whose name is Love."

The Enneagram offers nine mirrors for self-reflection. If we choose to gaze into them directly, they can help us shake loose of our illusions that lead us away from home in the first place.

> ➤ Type One strives for principled excellence as moral duty.
> ➤ Type Two strives for lavish love through self-sacrifice.
> ➤ Type Three strives for appreciative recognition through curated successes.
> ➤ Type Four strives for discovery of identity for faithful authenticity.
> ➤ Type Five strives for decisive clarity through thoughtful conclusions.
> ➤ Type Six strives for steady constancy through confident loyalty.
> ➤ Type Seven strives for imaginative freedom for inspirational independence.
> ➤ Type Eight strives for impassioned intensity for unfettered autonomy.
> ➤ Type Nine strives for harmonious peacefulness as congruent repose.

We can also view these nine pathways by the intrinsic needs they represent.

Type One	The Need to Be Perfect
Type Two	The Need to Be Needed
Type Three	The Need to Succeed
Type Four	The Need to Be Special (or Unique)
Type Five	The Need to Perceive (or Understand)
Type Six	The Need to Be Sure/Certain (or Secure)
Type Seven	The Need to Avoid Pain
Type Eight	The Need to Be Against
Type Nine	The Need to Avoid

"The nine explorations of the soul are pilgrimages unto themselves, consecrated and prayerful voyages with focused intentions."

- How is your type's need expressed in your life and relationships?

  _____

  _____

  _____

  _____

- What underlying fear drives your need?

  _____

  _____

  _____

  _____

HOW YOUR SOUL WAS PURPOSED

Another approach to understanding the nine types involves the purest features of each type—the Holy Ideas and Virtues. The Holy Idea of each type is the *mental clarity* of the True Self that emerges when the mind is at rest, while the Virtue of each type is the *emotional objectivity* of the True Self that comes forward in a heart at peace (page 36).

Together, your Holy Idea and Virtue express who you were always created to be and reveal the gift of your life—a unique way you bring healing to the world. They form the first truth you tell about yourself and your place in the world.

- What Holy Idea and Virtue pairing do you most identify with, and why do you feel drawn to them?

  _____

  _____

  _____

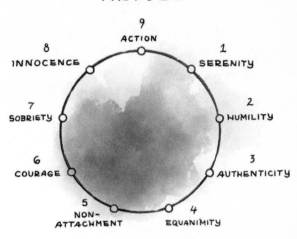

- Where have you seen your Holy Idea and Virtue show up in your life? What was going on around and in you?

_____

_____

_____

_____

_____

- What does your Holy Idea and Virtue tell you about the gifts you can bring to the people around you?

_____

_____

_____

_____

_____

- How can the truth of your Holy Idea and Virtue help you meet your type's need?

_____

_____

_____

_____

ATTACKS ON OUR VIRTUE

At some point in our early years, we all experienced a resistance to our Virtue, to the essence of our true self. And in light of that pain, we developed a False Self—reflex patterns that protect ourselves against the pain we don't want to face, and a way to feed the needs we fear will never be met. But these patterns often become harmful compulsions in the end.

The Enneagram reveals the nine ways our human nature uses such compulsions or addictions to protect the pain of our Childhood Wound. This attack on our virtue—either from individuals in our lives or from experiences of living in an imperfect world—lead us to lose contact with our True Self.

- How did you experience this wounding as a child? How does this pain continue to affect your choices and behavior today?

_____

_____

_____

_____

_____

_____

_____

_____

- How did you learn to cope with the pain when you were young? How do you continue to use those coping mechanisms?

_____

_____

_____

_____

_____

_____

_____

- What character growth would be available to you if you learned to set those coping methods aside?

  _____

  _____

  _____

  _____

  _____

  _____

  _____

- Read John 9:1–3 on page 55. What does this story reveal to you about how God views your life? Consider how your life story offers the opportunity for God's restoration to be made manifest.

  _____

  _____

  _____

  _____

  _____

  _____

  _____

DISCUSSION QUESTION

- Together in a group (or with a friend), share what you have learned about your Holy Idea and Virtue, including how you experienced resistance and learned to cope. Notice what thoughts and feelings you had as others in the group shared this information with you. What would it look like for you to view your own life story with the same compassion as you've felt for others?

  _____

  _____

  _____

  _____

  _____

Invitation

Welcoming Prayer

The welcoming prayer is a helpful practice that reveals the opportunities within your body to consent to God's truth and presence while intentionally letting go of thoughts and feelings that support a false-self system. Originally developed by Mary Mrozowski, a founder of Contemplative Outreach, the welcoming prayer invites you to practice gratitude for your body, heal the emotional wounds we tend to hold in our body, and journey a little closer to your true self.

To Begin

- Posture is the first gift you bring. As you are able, sit upright with your feet planted on the ground. Find a position that is attentive and restful. Start to deepen your breath—inhaling through your nose, holding it gently, then exhaling it through your mouth.
- Begin to bring your attention to this moment and God's presence.

Focus

- Slowly and intentionally, draw your focus to each member of your body in turn, beginning with your feet and moving all the way to the crown of your head. Offer gratitude to God for the gift of your body. As you find aches and soreness, receive it with thanks for the daily work your body does for you. Continue to breathe deeply as you sit at peace with your body.

Welcome

- Allow your focus to settle on any area of your body that seems uncomfortable or unbalanced. Perhaps you sense nervousness in your stomach, tightness in your shoulders, weakness in your back, or tension in your temples or jaw. Bring your attention to it and, rather than resisting, welcome it. Invite God into the feelings, thoughts, and sensations you have here and consider what this discomfort is telling you about your fear, sense of control, lack of trust, or anxiety.

- Continue to breathe deeply and consider what thoughts, fears, or emotions you need to release. Let them go by repeating something like, "I let go of the desire for security, affection, and control," and "I let go of the desire to change this feeling or sensation."
- When you feel the intensity of the discomfort or emotion subside, return to your breath and the present moment. Give thanks to God for spiritual healing and peaceful presence.

— 2 —

The Sacred Enneagram:
Chapter 5

Discovering Your Type

Before digging into the details of discerning your type, it's important to remember that *your type is yours to bring forward.* Because the shaping of our type is partially confirmed to us though the experience of our Childhood Wound, or attack on our Virtue, learning about our type can be a painful process. Your personal discovery of your own type is the key to opening the sacred map of the Enneagram and propelling you into growth.

There are three common strategies for discerning your type (page 60).

ONLINE TESTS

As the most popular strategy, there are several online tests that serve as a suitable place to begin exploring your type. The respected and recommended test is the Enneagram Institute's RHETI test. There is a small fee, but it is widely regarded as the most accurate, thorough, and time-tested online method. A shorter but also recommended test is available on the EnneaApp, which can be downloaded to your smartphone. Whatever online test you choose, try not to force a specific result but rather focus on answering each question as honestly as possible.

MEET WITH A TRAINED PROFESSIONAL

A trained professional will offer an excellent typing process through a one-on-one conversation called a typing interview. This method can take up to an hour and may require payment for the professional's time and expertise. You may find this option particularly helpful if you feel stuck between two types and would like help navigating common mistypings. To further explore this option, visit the Gravity Center at gravitycenter.com/enneagram-specialists/.

DO YOUR OWN RESEARCH

Most experts agree that if you are honest with yourself, reading the thorough descriptions of each number is a sufficient method for determining your Enneagram type. This method requires a level of maturity, self-awareness, and truthfulness. A good rule of thumb is that the description that makes you feel the most exposed or uncomfortable is usually the right one.

THE KEY TO THE ENNEAGRAM MAP

As we unfold the map of the Enneagram, everything we've intuitively known about ourselves is finally illuminated and put into words. The components that shape your type are: Holy Idea, Virtue, Childhood Wound, Basic Desire, Basic Fear, Passion, and Fixation (page 108).

Think of the chart on the next page as the map key to the Enneagram. In it we see the formation of each type's personality. This chart shows our true essence, those early days we may not totally remember but nevertheless gave us a sense that the world actually seemed okay. But something happened. We experienced an attack on our Holy Idea and Virtue and became disconnected from our essence. This created in us a Basic Desire, an unconscious aspiration to get back home to our True Self. Though good and holy in and of itself, this Basic Desire becomes warped by our uncertainty that we'll ever be able to go home and the fear that we are forever stuck in our flawed human experience.

Virtue Structure

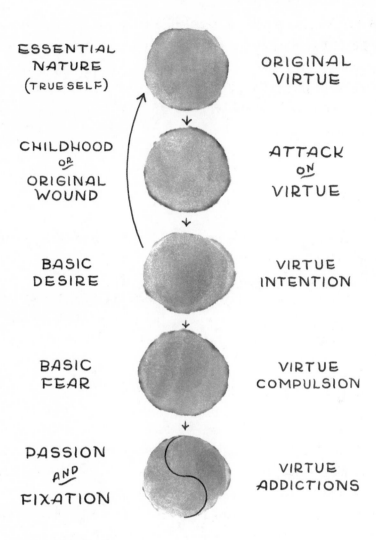

ESSENTIAL NATURE (TRUE SELF)   ORIGINAL VIRTUE

CHILDHOOD or ORIGINAL WOUND   ATTACK on VIRTUE

BASIC DESIRE   VIRTUE INTENTION

BASIC FEAR   VIRTUE COMPULSION

PASSION and FIXATION   VIRTUE ADDICTIONS

This tension then feeds into our Basic Fear and is experienced as our Virtue Compulsion. Like all fears, our Basic Fear is as powerful as we allow it to be. When we witness the illusionary power of the fears of others, our hearts often break for them. But we're convinced our fear is real.

To deal with this fear and the consequences of the attack on our essence, we lean into our Passions, how the heart suffers the disconnect from its True Self, and our Fixations, the mental tactics we use to support our Passion.

All of this can help us better understand the patterns of our False Self and how it has been developed over the course of a lifetime.

- When you think about your true essence, what words, feelings, or mental pictures come to mind?

_____

_____

_____

_____

_____

_____

_____

_____

_____

- The attack on our Virtue might have been a specific painful event, or it may have been the perceived lesson from a series of experiences. More often, the attack on our Virtue settles in after we experience our caregiver's inability to love us perfectly, coupled with our inability to perfectly receive love. As best as you can in a few sentences, articulate the attack on your Virtue.

_____

_____

_____

_____

_____

_____

_____

> "Learning to see ourselves for who we truly are—the good, the bad, the ugly—is a gift of grace."

OVERVIEW OF THE NINE TYPES

Type One (page 113)

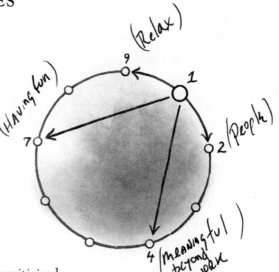

Holy Idea: Holy Perfection

Virtue: Serenity

Basic Desire: To be good, to have integrity

Basic Fear: Being bad, imbalanced, defective, corrupt

Fixation: Resentment

Passion: Anger

Direction of Integration: Type Seven

Direction of Disintegration: Type Four

Attack on Virtue: As children, Ones felt heavily criticized, punished, or not good enough. Household rules may have felt inconsistent. As such, they became obsessed with being good or not making mistakes to avoid condemnation. The principle message was "You always must be better than you are."

Communication Style: Generally instructive

Most likely of all the types to answer every single question in this workbook.

Strongly principled and committed to what, and who, they know is right and good.

Can't help but see things that need fixing or attention—like correcting how the dishwasher is loaded or noticing paint chips on the wall.

Have a knack for organization and efficiency and they pursue opportunities for excellence.

Feel as if they are trapped in a cell with a demanding idealist and struggle with the constant voice of their inner critic.

Fear they are inherently corrupt despite all their efforts.

Hold resentment against themselves for all their flaws and then turn the resentment outward to their external world. To others, this frustration can come across as judgmental.

Champions of justice and fairness.

Type Two (page 117)

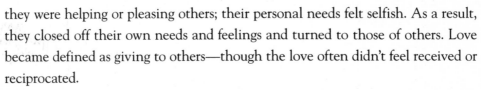

Holy Idea: Holy Will, Holy Freedom

Virtue: Humility

Basic Desire: To feel love

Basic Fear: Being unloved

Fixation: Flattery

Passion: Pride

Direction of Integration: Type Four

Direction of Disintegration: Type Eight

Attack on Virtue: These children felt loved only if they were helping or pleasing others; their personal needs felt selfish. As a result, they closed off their own needs and feelings and turned to those of others. Love became defined as giving to others—though the love often didn't feel received or reciprocated.

Communication Style: Dynamic one-on-one, mentor, consulting

Already saw and met a friend's need before that friend knew they had a need.

Believe they are only loved by what they give, not who they are.

Their hearts ache for the needs they intuitively recognize in others.

Genuinely interested in and remembers little details about the lives of those around them.

Worry that their relationships are based on transactions rather than genuine connection and fear that they come across as manipulative.

May not be aware of their needs and can feel stressed when asked to articulate their needs.

Convince or flatter themselves through false humility that their self-sacrifice is loving.

Naturally know how to love others well and see opportunities to serve and help—like doing the dishes at a friend's house or always serving as host.

Type Three (page 120)

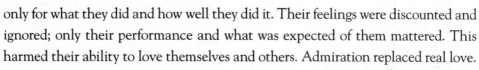

Holy Idea: Holy Harmony, Holy Law, Holy Hope

Virtue: Truthfulness, Authenticity

Basic Desire: To feel valuable

Basic Fear: Being worthless

Fixation: Vanity

Passion: Deceit

Direction of Integration: Type Six

Direction of Disintegration: Type Nine

Attack on Virtue: As children, Threes felt rewarded only for what they did and how well they did it. Their feelings were discounted and ignored; only their performance and what was expected of them mattered. This harmed their ability to love themselves and others. Admiration replaced real love.

Communication Style: Self-promoting but in a subtle, self-deprecating way

Think that even failure can look like success in the right light.

Fill their need for love with achievements and awards.

See value in everything and have an intuitive sense for recognizing when real authenticity is present.

Naturally discern what a group or team needs in order to be successful, and pivot and shape themselves into that missing role so well that they believe their social role is their identity.

Dissimulate the truth of who they are and share the pieces that are most helpful with others based on the needs around them.

Are driven to prove their value, which results in a competitive and determined nature and a strong work ethic.

Feel that no one knows the full story of who they truly are.

Often find themselves leading others in both obvious and unassuming ways.

Type Four (page 122)

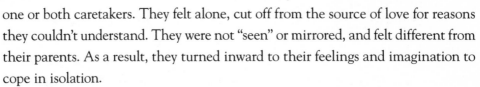

Holy Idea: Holy Origin

Virtue: Equanimity, Emotional Balance

Basic Desire: To be themselves

Basic Fear: Having no identity or significance

Fixation: Melancholy

Passion: Envy

Direction of Integration: Type One

Direction of Disintegration: Type Two

Attack on Virtue: These children felt abandoned by one or both caretakers. They felt alone, cut off from the source of love for reasons they couldn't understand. They were not "seen" or mirrored, and felt different from their parents. As a result, they turned inward to their feelings and imagination to cope in isolation.

Communication Style: Lucid, specific, and intentional

Possess a highly developed ability to see beauty and uniqueness in all things and people.

Have an eye for the refined, unique, and dramatic, and apply this to their work and relationships.

Know they are intrinsically different but also fear they are somehow less significant than others.

Project externally the search for significance that they feel internally. They long to be understood and are constantly looking for someone who sees them as they truly are.

Perceive that others experience more intimacy, meaning, and satisfaction than they do.

Secretly worry that their friends and family will abandon them.

Articulated sense of emotional intelligence and often have more language for their feelings than other types.

Comfortable with the depth and spectrum of emotions where other types feel overwhelmed.

Type Five (page 125)

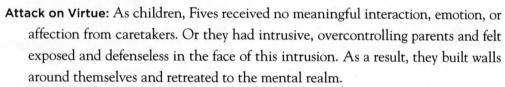

Holy Idea: Holy Omniscience, Holy Transparency

Virtue: Detachment (traditional), alternatively Non-Attachment

Basic Desire: To be capable and competent

Basic Fear: Being helpless, incompetent, and incapable

Fixation: Stinginess

Passion: Avarice

Direction of Integration: Type Eight

Direction of Disintegration: Type Seven

Attack on Virtue: As children, Fives received no meaningful interaction, emotion, or affection from caretakers. Or they had intrusive, overcontrolling parents and felt exposed and defenseless in the face of this intrusion. As a result, they built walls around themselves and retreated to the mental realm.

Communication Style: Informative, paragraph or report form

Most likely chose to buy this book in lieu of attending an Enneagram class with strangers.

Naturally curious and lifelong learners, they prefer to research on their own because their minds outpace the typical classroom or lecture format.

Intrinsically afraid they do not possess the capacity within themselves to distinguish or understand reality.

Highly self-contained and self-reliant and value self-reliance in others.

Often come across as minimalists to others but cultivate a complex mental life.

Hold more boundaries than others and are very careful how and with whom they spend their energy.

Compelled to collect data and preoccupied with how things fit together, which leads them to be slow at making decisions (including determining their Enneagram type).

More comfortable with thoughts than emotions and require time and reflection to discern what they're feeling.

Type Six (page 128)

Holy Idea: Holy Strength, Holy Faith

Virtue: Courage

Basic Desire: To have support and guidance

Basic Fear: Being without support and guidance

Fixation: Cowardice

Passion: Fear

Direction of Integration: Type Nine

Direction of Disintegration: Type Three

Attack on Virtue: These children were raised in an unpredictable situation with no safe place to go. They lost faith they would ever be protected. As such, they turned to their own inner defense of doubting—disbelieving reality and rejecting their own instincts and inner guidance.

Communication Style: Problem solving, warm and friendly

Amazing in a crisis and highly supportive of the people they are committed to.

Suspicious of authority figures and hidden agendas but do not necessarily want to assume leadership roles. They seek assurance that whoever is leading is the appropriate person for that role.

Doubt their own mind and often seek the advice and suggestions of others to affirm their ideas.

What sounds like fearful language to others is actually the inner courage of Sixes at work sensing potential risk and danger and formulating solutions and back-up plans.

Love others by doubling down on worst case scenarios, mentally going to the scariest places they can imagine so they can protect their friends and family.

Experience the constant hum of anxiety and angst in their minds and tend toward irrational overthinking processes.

Very loyal and friendly, often serve as a source of strength, security, and stability to others.

Type Seven (page 130)

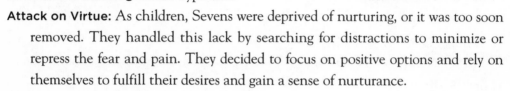

Holy Idea: Holy Wisdom, Holy Work, Holy Plan

Virtue: Sobriety

Basic Desire: To be satisfied

Basic Fear: Being trapped in pain and deprivation

Fixation: Planning

Passion: Gluttony

Direction of Integration: Type Five

Direction of Disintegration: Type One

Attack on Virtue: As children, Sevens were deprived of nurturing, or it was too soon removed. They handled this lack by searching for distractions to minimize or repress the fear and pain. They decided to focus on positive options and rely on themselves to fulfill their desires and gain a sense of nurturance.

Communication Style: Spontaneous and illustrative

Energetic and perpetually planning and anticipating the next exciting thing.

Have a knack for finding the silver lining in difficult situations.

Fast-thinking, quick on their feet, and often bored in groups or classrooms.

Self-nurturing posture which causes them to long for and feast on any activities and behaviors that give them gratification.

Find it difficult to articulate negative feelings and don't want to dwell on their emotions long enough to do so.

Prioritize and value freedom; experience fear and anxiety when they feel trapped with no exit route or alternative options.

Often find it hard to finish or follow through on projects because it feels like a loss and an ending, or an annoyance because they've already moved on.

Overall optimistic in nature and bring spontaneity, joy, and positivity to relationships.

Type Eight (page 133)

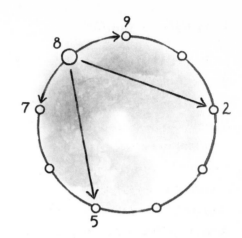

Holy Idea: Holy Truth

Virtue: Innocence

Basic Desire: To protect themselves

Basic Fear: Being harmed, controlled, and violated

Fixation: Vengeance

Passion: Lust

Direction of Integration: Type Two

Direction of Disintegration: Type Five

Attack on Virtue: These children often grew up in an unsafe environment (emotionally or physically) and had to mature way too soon. They didn't feel safe to show any vulnerability and may have felt controlled. Weakness was used against them, so they focused only on building their strength.

Communication Style: Bold, matter-of-fact, empowering

Source of initiating energy, strength, and vitality in the world.

Highly opinionated, sometimes just for the sake of getting reactions.

Extremists in their positions, vocations, and causes they champion.

With a knack for sensing when people are not being real with them, Eights shock or challenge boundaries first so they don't have to experience rejection later.

Push and fight others as a way to build trust in their relationships, testing whether others will stand up to them by standing up for themselves.

Fear being destroyed and being controlled, and resist anything that makes them slow down, feel interrupted, or cut off.

Overdo anything that makes them feel alive, even if it leads to self-harm.

Often find themselves letting down their guard around children and pets where there is no threat of control, and are drawn to defending the cause of the vulnerable.

Type Nine (page 136)

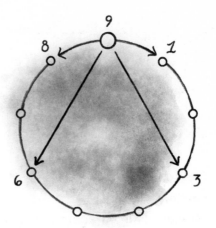

Holy Idea: Holy Love

Virtue: Action

Basic Desire: Peace of mind and wholeness

Basic Fear: Loss, separation, and fragmentation

Fixation: Indolence

Passion: Sloth

Direction of Integration: Type Three

Direction of Disintegration: Type Six

Attack on Virtue: As children, Nines were overlooked or neglected and felt unimportant or "lost." They were ignored or attacked for having needs or expressing themselves (especially anger) and decided to keep a low profile and instead focus on the needs and experiences of others.

Communication Style: Low key, suggestive, agreeable

Naturally calm and cool, and they bring a sense of tranquility and acceptance to their relationships.

Innately understand multiple perspectives and often find themselves in mediating roles.

Nines minimize their needs and prefer to focus on the needs of others, often caring and serving others in ways that go unnoticed.

Detach and withdraw to protect themselves from drama and energy requirements, even to the point of withdrawing from themselves.

Fear the disruption of their internal peace and stability and become stubbornly resistant if they feel encroached upon.

Takes a lot of energy for Nines to transition from a lethargic, self-forgetting, or procrastinating posture to action, but once they do, things get done.

Rarely show the anger they suppress but when they can't hold it anymore, their anger comes out suddenly, surprising everyone including themselves.

> "This knowledge is really just the beginning. And where we go from here reveals our willingness to press into our inner life, no matter how hard it may be."

QUESTIONS FOR REFLECTION

- What about your type do you find most compelling or interesting?

  _____

  _____

  _____

  _____

  _____

  _____

  _____

- What do you find difficult, uncomfortable, or embarrassing about your type?

  _____

  _____

  _____

  _____

  _____

  _____

- What do you value most about your Enneagram number?

  _____

  _____

  _____

  _____

  _____

  _____

- What does your type reveal about what you seek in your work?

  _____

  _____

  _____

  _____

  _____

- What does your type reveal about what you seek in your relationships?

  _____

  _____

  _____

  _____

  _____

- What does your Enneagram type show about the expectations you have for yourself?

  _____

  _____

  _____

  _____

  _____

- According to your type, how have you seen your response to fear, anxiety, and stress play out in your life?

  _____

  _____

  _____

  _____

  _____

- What do you wish people understood about what it's like to be you?

  _____

  _____

  _____

  _____

  _____

• How would you like to grow toward wholeness in your type?

_____

_____

_____

_____

_____

_____

DISCUSSION QUESTION

• Take turns sharing your type with the rest of the group. As each person introduces their type, briefly thank them and share how you've experienced a strength or gift they have through their type.

_____

_____

_____

_____

_____

_____

Invitation

In the space provided on page 42, write out the story of your personality with the Virtue Structure chart as a guide. Don't worry about using Enneagram terms or proper language. This is *your* story.

Virtue Structure

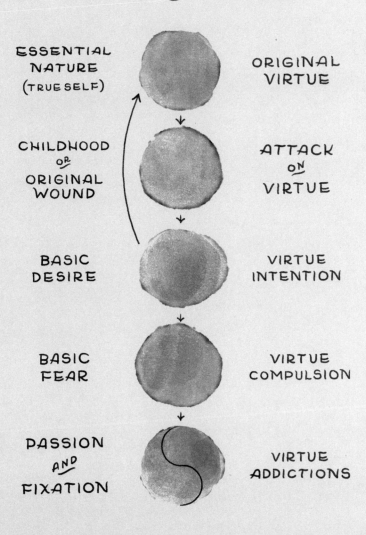

ESSENTIAL NATURE (TRUE SELF)	ORIGINAL VIRTUE
CHILDHOOD or ORIGINAL WOUND	ATTACK on VIRTUE
BASIC DESIRE	VIRTUE INTENTION
BASIC FEAR	VIRTUE COMPULSION
PASSION and FIXATION	VIRTUE ADDICTIONS

Write as much or as little as is comfortable, but try to give an overview from your early childhood days to your present self. This doesn't have to be shared with anyone else unless you'd like to share it. The goal is to give yourself an opportunity to begin the process of exploring and owning your personality narrative in your own words.

_____

_____

_____

_____

_____

_____

_____

_____

_____

_____

_____

_____

_____

_____

_____

_____

_____

_____

_____

_____

_____

_____

_____

_____

_____

The Sacred Enneagram:
Chapter 3

Identifying Your Patterns of Growth and Stress

INTEGRATION

DISINTEGRATION

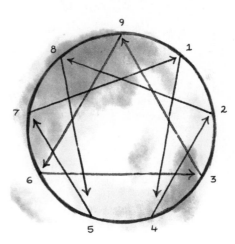

An essential component to unlocking personal development through the Enneagram is found in the crisscrossing lines which show each type's movement between states of health and unhealth. This is where we encounter the Enneagram's unique paths for growth because it prompts us to honestly identify how we function on the spectrum between wholeness and self-sabotage (page 66).

> "Our growth and stress point may vary from day to day or even
> hour to hour, but the gift presented to us is greater awareness
> that leads to psychological and spiritual growth."

It is important to note that we do not *become* the type that we integrate toward; it is only as we become a healthy, centered version of our dominant type that we are simultaneously able to reach across the Enneagram and "borrow" positive traits from our Heart Point. Integration is a surprising benefit from the faithful work of nourishing our soul. And the path is found not through forcing ourselves into another type but by accepting the best of ourselves *in* our dominant type (page 68).

Disintegration is better understood as our type's innate self-survival reflex when stressed—the self-preservation instinct similar to reaching out and grabbing what we can find when we sense that we're falling. Through self-awareness, we learn to see our path of disintegration as the natural warning sign that it is, not a condemnation but a guide pointing back toward home (page 70).

Integration and disintegration are terms for the dynamic, natural movement of our personalities. And some developing concepts suggest that we can also take on the strong and weak traits of both wings.

- What is your type's path of integration and disintegration?

  _____

  _____

  _____

  _____

  _____

- What does integration look like for you? What traits do you borrow and how do you utilize them?

  _____

  _____

  _____

  _____

- What does disintegration look like for you? What traits do you borrow and how do you utilize them?

  _____

  _____

  _____

  _____

  _____

- What types of situations, feelings, or thoughts trigger your path toward disintegration?

  _____

  _____

  _____

  _____

- What types of situations, feelings, or thoughts set you up for integration?

  _____

  _____

  _____

  _____

The Enneagram shows us the unique patterns and behavioral loops which keep us stuck. At the root of nearly every decision we make is our desire to find our way back home to our essential nature and back to God. But the reality of living in a broken world means that we often go about this in all the wrong ways. This shows up in our lives in our Passions and Fixations (page 71).

	Mind/Heart Center	**Heart/Feeling Center**
Centered	Holy Idea = Mental Clarity	Virtue = Emotional Objectivity
Uncentered	Fixation = Mental Hyperactivity	Passion = Emotional Reactivity

(page 73)

The shadow of each type's Holy Idea is the Fixation—how the mind copes with the True Self's loss of perfection and presence. And the shadow of the Virtue is each type's Passion—how the heart aches and longs to reconnect with the Virtue of the True Self (page 73).

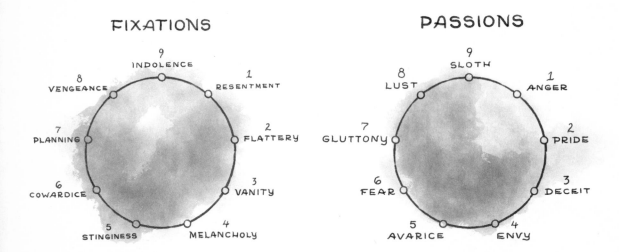

In unhealth, some of us will become so preoccupied with our Fixations and Passions that we lose sight of our true gifts and contributions. Though naming and taking responsibility for our Passion is devastating to the ego and can be extremely painful, taking ownership of our Passion also leads to tremendous growth (page 76). By practicing self-compassion, we can view our Passion as the unique way our heart suffers the disconnect from its True Self and see it as the invitation to return to true Virtue.

> "We are punished by our sins not for them."
> —*American philosopher Elbert Hubbard*

- How has the quote above proved true in your life?

_____

_____

_____

_____

- What is your type's Passion and Fixation? What feelings and thoughts arise in you with this knowledge?

  _____

  _____

  _____

  _____

  _____

  _____

- When you feel trapped between your Passion and Fixation, what gifts and contributions are unfortunately forgotten or pushed aside?

  _____

  _____

  _____

  _____

  _____

  _____

- How has your Fixation influenced your decisions and relationships?

  _____

  _____

  _____

  _____

  _____

  _____

- How does your Passion influence your behavior?

  _____

  _____

  _____

  _____

  _____

  _____

- How has your Fixation and Passion influenced your relationship with God?

  _____

  _____

  _____

  _____

  _____

  _____

- When your Fixation and Passion show up again in your life, how might you be able to lean into your Holy Idea and Virtue?

  _____

  _____

  _____

  _____

  _____

  _____

DISCUSSION QUESTION

- Review the parable of The King's Diamond (pages 79–81) and discuss how this story applies to the relationship between your True Self and your Passions and Fixations. Reflect on what this story illuminates about God's power of transformation and reconciliation.

  _____

  _____

  _____

  _____

  _____

Invitation

Repeated Questions

Set a timer for three minutes and ask yourself the question corresponding to your type number. Jot down the answer that comes to you and then repeat the process. This practice works best when done somewhat quickly, so try not to overthink or reflect too long. Simply write down the first answer that occurs, and then ask yourself the question again until the timer sounds.

Afterward, reflect on the experience and the thoughts and feelings you had. Consider what your answers revealed to you about yourself. Hold compassion for yourself and all that you've experienced. Appreciate with gratitude the hard work you are doing in this journey toward growth.

Type One. What is good about yourself?

_____
_____
_____
_____
_____
_____
_____
_____

Type Two. What do you need?

_____
_____
_____
_____
_____
_____
_____

Type Three. What do you expect from yourself?

_____
_____
_____
_____
_____
_____
_____

Type Four. What is special about your life now?

_____
_____
_____
_____
_____
_____
_____

Type Five. What drives your need for information?

_____
_____
_____
_____
_____
_____
_____

Type Six. How do you trust yourself?

_____
_____
_____
_____
_____
_____

Type Seven. How do you handle your painful emotions?

_____

_____

_____

_____

_____

_____

_____

Type Eight. How are you vulnerable?

_____

_____

_____

_____

_____

_____

_____

Type Nine. How are you valuable?

_____

_____

_____

_____

_____

_____

PART II

GOING DEEPER
into YOUR
ENNEAGRAM
JOURNEY

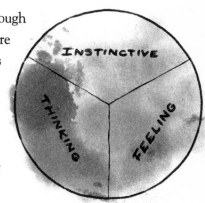

— 4 —

The Sacred Enneagram:
Chapter 4

Intelligence Centers

Each Enneagram type primarily perceives the world through the head, heart, or body. These Intelligence Centers are activated through our involuntarily physiological reactions and responses to every experience. A deep awareness and familiarity with our center is key to helping us develop discernment, which in turn enables us to perceive what is true, make good decisions, and know how best to act. Ultimately, it's discernment that helps us receive and listen to the loving presence and voice of God (pages 88–90).

> "We already know how to practice discernment,
> and it starts with self-awareness."

These Intelligence Centers serve as the basis for our understanding of how the world works and how we work in the world. These include:

The Body Center—instinctive, gut—Types Eight, Nine, and One

The Heart Center—feeling, emotion—Types Two, Three, and Four

The Head Center—mind, thinking, rational—Types Five, Six, and Seven

Our use of discernment relies on the clarity of our centered minds, the objectivity of peace-filled hearts, and the unobstructed instincts of our bodies (page 88). Our Intelligence Center is the innate gift that indicates how God speaks to us—through the impressions we experience in either our instincts, feelings, or thoughts (page 91).

- What thoughts and feelings do you have about the truth that you have already been gifted with everything you need to discern God's voice in your life?

_____

_____

_____

_____

_____

_____

- How have you discerned God's voice in the past?

_____

_____

_____

_____

_____

_____

- What does your type's Intelligence Center tell you about the specific way that God made you to connect with God's presence?

_____

_____

_____

_____

_____

_____

• How does your Intelligence Center enable you to understand others?

_____

_____

_____

_____

_____

_____

_____

• How does your Intelligence Center enable you to understand yourself?

_____

_____

_____

_____

_____

_____

_____

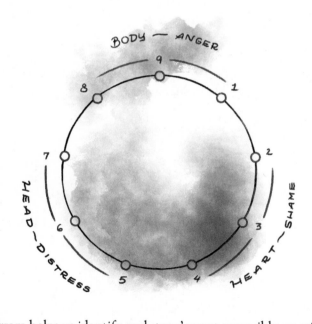

The Enneagram helps us identify each type's most accessible emotional response or reaction: anxiety or distress for the Head Center, fear or shame for the Heart Center, and frustration or anger for the Body Center.

- What is it like to experience your type's emotional response?

  _____

  _____

  _____

  _____

  _____

  _____

  _____

- What situations, sensations, impressions, feelings, or thoughts trigger this experience?

  _____

  _____

  _____

  _____

  _____

  _____

  _____

- How might you release this distress, shame, or anger in a healthy way so that it doesn't overwhelm you and negatively impact others?

  _____

  _____

  _____

  _____

  _____

  _____

  _____

> "Love the Most High God with all your heart, with all
> your soul, and with all your mind."
> —*Matthew 22:37*

THE HEAD CENTER

Those with dominant types in the Head Center believe that by mastering their environment, they can secure their own self-preservation. Fives analyze everything to predict the future through research and proper understanding. Sixes live on constant alert and attempt to cut off any threat through contingency planning. Sevens feel an inner compulsion to maintain access to opportunity as a way of experiencing freedom (page 93).

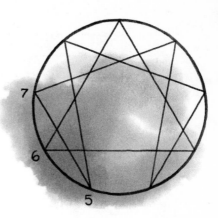

HEAD~INTELLECTUAL~THINKING

THE HEART CENTER

At their core, those with an emotional Intelligence Center project their fears of not being loved, valued, or seen through quiet attempts to have their own needs met: Twos want to be loved for who they are not what they do for others; Threes are concerned they're more admired than loved; Fours worry that they'll never be loved for what sets them apart as special (page 95).

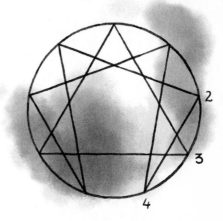

HEART~FEELING~EMOTION

THE BODY CENTER

People in the Body Center engage the world through activity in an effort to assert and maintain a sense of control. Externalizing their interior irritations, gut people assert their desire for control by becoming the solution to the drama they perceive: Eights dominate it, Nines attempt to broker it, and Ones seek to bring back balance by correcting it (page 97).

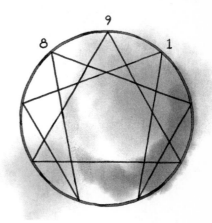

BODY~GUT~INSTINCTIVE

• In unhealth, how have you reacted to stressful or uncomfortable situations through your Intelligence Center?

_____

_____

_____

_____

_____

• What times, places, people, or situations trigger unhealthy patterns for you?

_____

_____

_____

_____

_____

• How have you reacted to situations in health and balance through your Intelligence Center?

_____

_____

_____

_____

_____

At their best, Head types trust that they already have all the information needed to be competent in the world; Heart types trust their emotional intuition which empowers them to bring balance and love to the world; and Body types trust their physical energy and initiation to make the world a better place (pages 93–98).

• How would your life be different if you trusted your type's Intelligence Center?

_____

_____

_____

_____

_____

Though we all have one dominant Intelligence Center, if we don't integrate the whole of who we are—mind, heart, and body—we miss the wholeness for which we were originally created. The more grounded you are in your center, the more the other two centers will support your dominant one (page 101).

- In times of health and strength, how might your dominant center lead you into the integration of your whole self?

_____

_____

_____

_____

_____

"Bringing our centers together through the inner work of integration helps us wake up and come home to our True Self."

DISCUSSION QUESTION

- Reflect or discuss how each Intelligence Center brings a unique expression of unity, wholeness, and the presence of the Divine into community. For Christians, how does this correspond with the Body of Christ?

_____

_____

_____

_____

Invitation

Lectio Divina

Lectio Divina, Latin for sacred reading, is an ancient monastic form of prayer and meditation. When paired with the Enneagram, this simple practice offers an opportunity to connect with the Divine through your Intelligence Center. All you need is a comfortable place to sit and access to Scripture, a sacred text, prayer book, poetry, or some other devotional text.

1. Take a minute to breathe deeply and turn the attention of your mind, heart, and body to the presence of divine love.
2. Read the selected Scripture or text, at least a sentence or two, and at most a few paragraphs. To start, you may like to select one of these passages: Psalm 1, Psalm 23, Mark 4:35–41, or Mark 8:22–25.
3. Take notice of a word or phrase that stirs an emotion, thought, or physical response in you.
4. Share your heartfelt response to God.
5. Rest in your experience with gratitude.

The Sacred Enneagram:
Chapter 6

Harmony Triads

Our Intelligence Centers illuminate how we *see* the world, and our Harmony Triads illuminate how we *relate* to, connect with, and engage the world. The wisdom of the Harmony Triads reveals additional patterns to human nature and is critical to our emotional, relational, and spiritual growth (page 142).

The Harmony Triads make up three distinct teams of three Enneagram Types. Each triad includes a Type dominant in each Intelligence Center—Head, Heart, and Body—and the teams are grouped together according to the affinities they share (page 143).

HARMONY TRIAD
RELATIONISTS

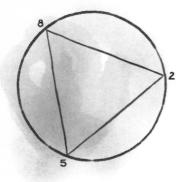

The Relationists		Relate to the world through connections.
	Type 2	Moves toward others to meet needs and give care.
✓	Type 5	Moves away from others to deliver reason and perspective.
	Type 8	Declarative with others, speaking out and asserting what is required.

HARMONY TRIAD
PRAGMATISTS

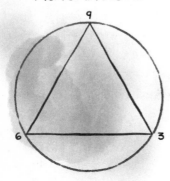

The Pragmatists		Relate to the world through their role.
	Type 3	Driven to perform a valuable and useful role.
	Type 6	Driven to assure a safe and secure existence in the world.
	Type 9	Driven to seek a comfortable position or place in the world.

HARMONY TRIAD
IDEALISTS

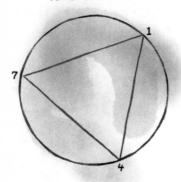

The Idealists		Relate to the world as it ought to be.
	Type 1	Seeks the perfect world according to internal standards.
	Type 7	Seeks the ideal positive world free of suffering and pain.
	Type 4	Seeks the ultimate ideal world where nothing of importance is missed.

- What patterns of relating to the world do you find reflected through your Harmony Triad?

  _____
  _____
  _____
  _____
  _____

- Consider the people you feel drawn to in most social settings, or who may be in the other two types in your Harmony Triad. How are your personalities similar and different?

  _____
  _____
  _____
  _____
  _____

- How we relate to the world is an expression of how we relate to the Divine. What does your Harmony Triad illuminate about your relationship with God?

  _____
  _____
  _____
  _____

Each Harmony Triad is led by the energy of its Heart Center type. Relationists relate to the world through connections, a dominant function of the heart-centered Type Two. Pragmatists relate to the world through what works, which is demonstrated in the accomplishments of the Three. And Idealists relate to the world through their dreams for a better world, and there's no greater dreamer than the Four (page 146).

> "To open the 'heart' of every type is an invitation to live life to the fullest.
> To live in a world that needs to be engaged through harmonious love."

- What might it look like for you to connect to and trust your heart?

  _____

  _____

  _____

  _____

  _____

- What challenges prevent you from "putting the mind in the heart" (page 148)?

  _____

  _____

  _____

  _____

  _____

- How do these challenges limit your access to your heart's spiritual perception (page 148)?

  _____

  _____

  _____

  _____

  _____

- What small, practical steps can you take this week to overcome these challenges?

  _____

  _____

  _____

  _____

  _____

Dominant Affect Groups lead us a step further by telling us how we relate to the world specifically as a result of our defining family relationships. Layering our Dominant Affect Group with our Harmony Triad can help us understand the reasons behind why we think, act, and feel as we do (page 151). Often these reasons trace back to our childhood environment and development.

Rejection Types

Type Two	Felt rejected because the nurturing love they offered their protective caregiver wasn't reciprocated, so overidentifies with nurturing energy.
Type Five	Rejected both the nurturing and protective caregivers as intrusive and withdrew to assume a self-nurturing and self-protective stance.
Type Eight	Felt controlled by the nurturing love they were offered by their caregiver and rejected it, so overidentifies with protective energy.

Attachment Types

Type Three	Attaches to the energy of the nurturing caregiver and subsequently becomes capable of self-nurturing.
Type Six	Attaches to the energy of the protective caregiver and subsequently becomes capable of self-protection.
Type Nine	Attaches to the energy of both the nurturing and protective caregivers and subsequently becomes capable of self-nurturing and self-protection.

Frustration Types

Type One	Frustrated that the protective caregiver didn't safeguard enough, so compensates by assuming a self-protective stance.
Type Four	Frustrated that the nurturing and protective caregivers didn't offer enough, so compensates by assuming self-protection and self-nurture.
Type Seven	Frustrated that the nurturing caregiver didn't nurture enough, so compensates by assuming a self-nurturing stance.

(page 151)

Though sometimes painful, understanding the truth of our early years can help us understand how we were affected by the accidents of not loving each other perfectly. And with this understanding can come space for reconciliation and healing.

- In your own words, how would you describe your response and reaction to your caregivers?

  _____

  _____

  _____

  _____

  _____

- How does this information influence the way you think about your caregivers now?

  _____

  _____

  _____

  _____

  _____

No matter where you find yourself in the Dominant Affect Groups, we all have an invitation to move toward wholeness.

- Rejection Types essentially reject what they most want in relationships. To grow, these Types must be truthful about their needs and cultivate a willingness for their needs to be met.

- Pragmatic Types attach to what works for them. To grow, they must recognize that they need to engage practical ways of nurturing their spirituality.

- Frustration Types are constantly irritated by their own idealism. To grow, they must recognize their desperate need to rest in God.

> "Giving ourselves to this path requires a disciplined cultivation of spiritual depth through faithful contemplative practice that brings us into the transforming presence of a loving God."

- What would it look like for your type to receive and put into practice your Dominant Affect Group's invitation to move toward wholeness?

_____

_____

_____

_____

_____

- In what ways have you already begun taking steps on the path toward growth? Take a moment to name and recognize your progress so far.

_____

_____

_____

_____

_____

DISCUSSION QUESTION

- How has your experience with your caregivers colored the way you understand God's love and care for you? How might a daily mindfulness, meditation, or contemplative practice help align your heart with God's?

_____

_____

_____

_____

Invitation

Centering Prayer

Centering Prayer is a contemplative practice that prepares us to receive the gift of experiencing the Divine's presence with us. Centering Prayer is grounded in relationship with God and is a practice to nurture that spiritual connection. This kind of intentional prayer is proven to increase mental, emotional, and physical well-being when practiced for twenty minutes, two times a day. But with all new practices, it's wise to start out slowly with five to ten minutes in prayer at first.

1. Sit in an upright, attentive posture which allows for an erect spine (as much as you are able) and an open heart. Place your hands in your lap.

2. Select a sacred word or image—such as *love*, *peace*, *belonging*, or the phrase *be still*—or hold in your mind a place that represents peace or connection with God—such as a location from your childhood or the memory of a safe place in your imagination.

3. Silently, and with eyes closed, consent and surrender yourself to the presence of God. Turn your yielded attention, your whole self, to the Divine.

4. Recall your sacred word or image. Whenever you notice your thoughts wandering, gently return your attention to your sacred focus.

5. As your prayer time comes to an end, allow yourself to transition to your active life with gentleness and grace.

YOUR UNIQUE PATH *to* SPIRITUAL GROWTH

The Sacred Enneagram:
Chapter 7

The Unexpected Gifts of Silence,
Solitude, and Stillness

The path to bringing the fragmented parts of our True Selves together into a vibrant whole is found through the practices of solitude, silence, and stillness. Through regular use, they invite us to consider new ways of praying—praying with our whole self—mind, heart, and body. In solitude, silence, and stillness, we find the invitation to rest our minds and open our hearts. We encounter our own coping mechanisms and the lies we believe about our personalities, and we experience the grace of letting go, of surrendering to the presence of God (pages 162–164).

> "Silence is God's first language."
> —*St. John of the Cross*

However, these daily practices of solitude, silence, and stillness rarely feel as blissful or dramatic as they may sound. Real transformation happens not in a single moment or pivotal event but in a lifelong series of small surrenders, which we might even call minor deaths, as we lower the shields of our coping mechanisms, let go of our self-illusions, and at last, come home to our True Self (page 166).

- Matthew 16:24 says, "If you wish to come after me, you must deny your very selves, take up the instrument of your own death and begin to follow in my footsteps." What do Jesus' words mean to you in light of what you've learned about the nature of your False Self and your True Self (page 166)?

  _____

  _____

  _____

  _____

  _____

- How might this series of minor deaths, setting down the unhealthy parts of ourselves in order to take up our True Self, resemble the resurrection and redemptive power of God at work in you?

  _____

  _____

  _____

  _____

  _____

> "The best way out is always through."
>
> —*Robert Frost*

Solitude, the intentional withdrawal, teaches us to be present to ourselves, to God, and with others. Silence helps us learn how to listen to the voice of God and the loving and truthful words of people close to us (page 171). Stillness teaches us restraint, where we are able to discern what appropriate engagement looks like.

The gifts of each of these contemplative practices not only nurture the inner spirituality of our souls and quiet the mind but also enable us to make corrections to our behaviors that were otherwise obscured by life's noises (page 172).

- How often would you honestly say you experience moments of silence, solitude, or stillness in your life right now? On a daily, weekly, and monthly basis?

_____

_____

_____

_____

_____

- What thoughts or feelings arise in you when you find yourself alone, without distractions, or waiting to do something?

_____

_____

_____

_____

- When you feel overwhelmed, exhausted, frustrated, or anxious, what activities and habits do you resort to in order to find relaxation or refreshment?

_____

_____

_____

_____

- Which of these activities and habits are helpful in giving you energy and peace and connecting you to God? Which ones are unhelpful?

_____

_____

_____

_____

"To the extent that we are transformed, the world is transformed."
—*Phileena Heuertz*

WHY CONTEMPLATIVE PRACTICE?

Christianity has strong, ancient roots in contemplative spirituality, which seeks to know and experience the loving presence of God in our here and now. After the modern church lost touch with these roots, many Christians have only now begun to discover the profound spiritual growth available to them through contemplative prayer.

Contemplative practice is so effective because it brings a gentle awakening to the unconscious, misguided, selfish, and ego-driven impulses buried within us. When we become aware of these hidden motivations, we are able to mitigate some of the unintended, yet still harmful consequences and do better.

Grounding our social actions in contemplative practice ensures both personal and community wholeness. And this happens by nurturing interior postures of solitude, silence, and stillness in our practice of prayer.

- If you only had three sentences to express your spiritual journey, what would you say? Try it here.

_____

_____

_____

_____

_____

- How have spiritual practices shaped you as a person? Which ones mean the most to you?

_____

_____

_____

_____

- How have these spiritual practices shaped your understanding of God?

_____

_____

_____

_____

STILLNESS, SOLITUDE, AND SILENCE

When we pair the self-awareness that the Enneagram offers with contemplative practices, we discover our own unique path to spiritual growth.

With the driving energy of Eights, the dedicated mediation of Nines, and the desire to fix all broken things of Ones, stillness prompts the question: Who am I without the good I do? The gift of stillness interrupts the addiction and drive to do and creates interior accountability for wholesome engagement in life (page 181).

For Twos who try to meet the needs of others, Threes who respond to the emotional energy of others, and Fours who long to be seen and appreciated by others, solitude prompts the question: Who am I when I'm alone? The gift of solitude corrects the Heart types' dependency on connection and comparisons and teaches us to be present to God, ourselves, and to others as our True Selves (page 182).

For Fives always searching for answers, Sixes constantly worrying, and Sevens who never cease planning the next adventure, silence prompts the question: Who am I when my mind is quiet? The gift of silence interrupts the constant interior monologue and teaches us how to listen to the voice of God, to our own hearts and bodies, and to the loving words of others.

STILLNESS

SOLITUDE

SILENCE

- In what ways do you resist the practices of solitude, silence, and stillness in your life?

  _____

  _____

  _____

  _____

  _____

  _____

  _____

- Reflect on the question prompted by your type's contemplative practice. What answer would you give?

  _____

  _____

  _____

  _____

  _____

  _____

- What does your answer to the previous question reveal about your self-illusion that you are what you do, what you have, or what others think about you?

  _____

  _____

  _____

  _____

  _____

  _____

"When we resist the reductionism of inner fragmentation, we realize we aren't as bad as our worst moments or as good as our greatest success—but that we are far better than we can imagine and carry the potential to be far worse than we fear."

- What feels uncomfortable or even scary about setting aside regular time for solitude, silence, or stillness?

_____

_____

_____

_____

- In what ways have you latched onto parts of yourself you think are valuable or attractive and pushed down parts of yourself that you think are less so? What would your life look like if you could accept yourself wholly (page 185)?

_____

_____

_____

_____

> "We need practices that open us to this grace, this work of God.
> God is love, and therefore God can be trusted. In these practices,
> God will do for us what we cannot do for ourselves."

"Desire"

Enneagram Intelligence Centers	Nouwen's Lies	Keating's Programs	Jesus' Temptations	Contemplative Prayer Posture	God's Affirmations
Gut/Body Type Eight Type Nine Type One	"I am what I do."	Power + Control	"Tell these stones to become bread."	Stillness (Engagement)	This is my beloved child.
Heart/Emotions Type Two Type Three Type Four	"I am what others say or think about me."	Affection + Esteem	"Throw yourself down."	Solitude (Presence)	Rest in the truth that you belong to me.
Head/Mind Type Five Type Six Type Seven	"I am what I have."	Security + Survival	"All this I will give you."	Silence (Listening)	My favor over you is all you need.

what "I/others" do not do, does not define "them/me"
what "I/others" do not have, does not define "them/me".

• When you reflect on God's Affirmation to the lie, program for happiness, or temptation of your type, what feelings and thoughts do you experience?

_____

_____

_____

_____

_____

• How might you begin to surrender and release these coping mechanisms and addictions and to accept wholeheartedly the divine truth within you? Name one step you can take today.

_____

_____

_____

_____

_____

DISCUSSION QUESTION

• Most of us understand that self-care and emotional and mental wellness are essential to living and loving well. And yet, as a culture, we find it so hard to regularly disconnect and make contemplative practices a priority. Reflect or discuss the challenges we face personally and culturally which prevent us from experiencing the gifts of solitude, silence, and stillness. Consider what steps can be taken, individually and as a group, to create space and time for these life-giving practices.

_____

_____

_____

_____

Invitation

Be Still

Resting in God's loving presence is one of the greatest gifts available to us. Psalm 46:10 says, "Be still and know that I am God." The goal of this contemplative practice is to quiet your body, mind, and heart until you are at a place of attentive rest and intentional stillness with God.

1. Find a quiet place where you can pray alone. Settle into a relaxing but attentive posture. Begin slowing your breath, inhaling through your nose and exhaling through your mouth.
2. After a few deep breaths and when you are ready, recite Psalm 46:10 in consecutive diminishing lines:

> Be still and know that I am God.
> Be still and know that I am.
> Be still and know.
> Be still.
> Be.

3. Continue breathing deeply and enjoy this space of stillness.
4. When you are ready, pray "Amen," and gently return to your day.

7

The Sacred Enneagram:
Chapters 8 and 9

Nine Journeys Home

The Enneagram helps awaken us to self-awareness which reveals what our particular type needs to come alive and thrive. Our Intelligence Center reveals how we see the world and our Harmony Triad reveals how we engage the world. Going a step further in our journey home, our Prayer Posture reveals the contemplative practice we need to correct our misperceptions of the world and find wholeness. Our Prayer Intention is the action we take to reconnect with God and our True Self (page 194).

	Harmony Triad	Prayer Posture	Prayer Intention
Type One	Idealist	Stillness	Rest
Type Two	Relationist	Solitude	Consent
Type Three	Pragmatist	Solitude	Engage
Type Four	Idealist	Solitude	Rest
Type Five	Relationist	Silence	Consent
Type Six	Pragmatist	Silence	Engage
Type Seven	Idealist	Silence	Rest
Type Eight	Relationist	Stillness	Consent
Type Nine	Pragmatist	Stillness	Engage

(page 195)

CONSENT

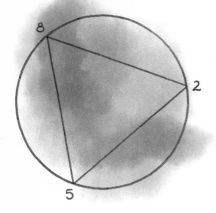

ENGAGE

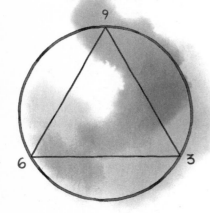

REST

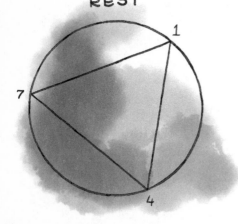

Consent, engagement, and rest are the intentions that help us find our way home. When these mindfulness intentions are combined with the postures of solitude, silence, and stillness, we start to wake up from our self-illusions (page 196).

Because Relationists avoid or reject their needs, their prayer invitation is consenting to the gift of having needs. More than mere acquiescence, consent is an active agreement to give of yourself in an offering of love. Consent is saying yes to what facilitates your coming home (page 197).

Because the Pragmatists hold on to what they desire, engagement is the prayer intention that loosens their grasp. Engagement is about simply showing up, intentionally being aware of our needs, and connecting to our Intelligence Center as we move toward wholeness and integration (page 199).

Because Idealists are perpetually frustrated with not being able to achieve their ideals, rest is the prayer intention that meets their deepest needs. Rest gives us the much-needed respite from our constant frustration and allows us to find the truth of who we are (page 200).

- When you read about your Prayer Intention, what thoughts, sensations, or feelings arose in you and why?

_____

_____

_____

_____

_____

_____

_____

_____

• Reflecting back on your life, when was the last time you experienced your type's Prayer Intention?

_____

_____

_____

_____

_____

_____

_____

_____

_____

• Consider all your internal reactions to what you've learned about your type so far. With this in mind, consider the question: What do you need most from God (page 196)?

_____

_____

_____

_____

_____

_____

_____

_____

• What does your type's Prayer Intention tell you about the gift God might be offering to your soul?

_____

_____

_____

_____

_____

_____

_____

CONTEMPLATIVE GROWTH FOR ENNEAGRAM TYPES

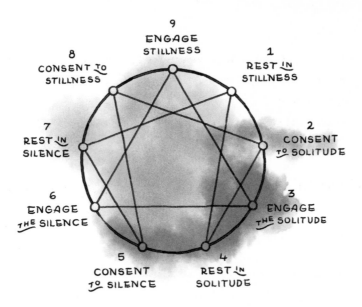

- When Ones rest in stillness, they are able to receive God's love as the ultimate source of the goodness they strive so hard to achieve.
- Twos who withdraw to solitude consent to be present to God rather than to please God, which allows them to be filled by God with the love they long for.
- By engaging solitude, Threes are able to face and accept themselves as they truly are in the present moment.
- When Fours rest in solitude, they allow themselves to take a break from their inner turmoil and come back to their relationships with clarity and emotional calm.
- Fives who consent to silence are able to set aside the perpetuating lie that freedom is found in answers and can rest in the truth that God will still be there in the mystery and when their mind is at rest.
- When Sixes engage silence as a way of overcoming fear and worry, they discover their inner courage.
- By resting in silence, Sevens allow themselves to be present and find the greatest adventures already lie within their own soul.
- Eights who consent to stillness make an agreement to stop and release their need to be in control and rather rest in their trust in God.

- When Nines engage stillness, they discover the conscious intention to show up and be present to God.

> "We lack presence because we are preoccupied with something in the future, fixated on the past, or regretting the inability to control the now. Contemplative practice roots our self in presence, which leads to balance and integrates our Head, Heart, and Body."

- Considering the quote above, how do you find that you most often lack presence?

_____

_____

_____

_____

_____

_____

- The way you judge yourself or fear that you'll somehow experience failure in contemplative practice is often the very thing that opens your type to the graces of contemplative practice (page 193). What might this mean for you?

_____

_____

_____

_____

_____

_____

> "As we give ourselves to contemplative practice, aligning prayer postures with intentions to support our spiritual growth, something happens to us. We find new ways of coming home."

MAPPING YOUR UNIQUE PATH TO SPIRITUAL GROWTH

The Way Home for One: *Rest in Stillness*

Intelligence Center	Body/Gut/Instinctive
Harmony Triad	Idealist
Dominant Affect Group	Frustration
Prayer Posture	Stillness
Prayer Intention	Rest
Passion	Anger
Fixation	Resentment
Holy Idea	Holy Perfection
Virtue	Serenity

The Challenge: Ones are driven to keep moving in order to fix all that is flawed; this notion drives them to the end of themselves. They are tempted to believe the lie that *they are what they do.* The constant monologue of their inner critic makes it challenging to reconnect with their original Virtue of Serenity and the grace of God.

The Invitation: It is crucial for Ones to learn self-compassion. By resting in stillness, Ones find their breath and let themselves off the hook for not always getting everything right; yet at the same time, they reconnect with the holy perfection in which everything belongs, even imperfections. Rest allows them to return to the gifts of the present moment in all the ways that nurture their spirituality. When Ones truly practice being still, they are able to dial down the driving movement, balance their energy, and renew the serenity of their True Self (page 208).

The Way Home for Two: *Consent to Solitude*

Intelligence Center	Heart/Feeling/Emotion
Harmony Triad	Relationist
Dominant Affect Group	Rejection
Prayer Posture	Solitude
Prayer Intention	Consent
Passion	Pride
Fixation	Flattery
Holy Idea	Holy Will, Freedom
Virtue	Humility

The Challenge: Twos live from the heart more than any other type, but it is difficult for Twos to connect with their own hearts because so much of their energy is focused on tending the hearts of others. Twos naturally fall into the lie that *they are what others think or say about them*, and they suffer this through the subconscious compulsion to form ever deeper, more intimate connections to prove they are worth loving. This drive makes it challenging to say yes to themselves and their needs and to receive the unconditional love of God.

The Invitation: Consenting to solitude is essential for Twos to unmask the lie and recenter themselves within their hearts. Agreeing to being alone in solitude confronts their addiction to giving themselves away, helps them to be honest about their needs, and enables them to be present with the gift and strength of their own self-defined identity. By intentionally choosing the gift of solitude, Twos learn to rest in the grace and freedom that they are loved not for what they do for the rest of us but for who they are (page 209).

The Way Home for Three: *Engage Solitude*

Intelligence Center	Heart/Feeling/Emotion
Harmony Triad	Pragmatist
Dominant Affect Group	Attachment
Prayer Posture	Solitude
Prayer Intention	Engage
Passion	Deceit
Fixation	Vanity
Holy Idea	Holy Harmony, Hope
Virtue	Truthfulness, Authenticity

The Challenge: Disconnected from their hearts, Threes almost seem to observe their feelings at arm's length. They are tethered to the addiction of pushing feelings aside because they think emotions are impractical or not sensible enough to aid in making clear decisions. They are tempted to believe that *they are what others think or say about them*, and they foster a malformed perception of love which casts the illusion that they will only be loved by gaining the admiration of others.

The Invitation: Solitude offers Threes a break from seeking the admiration of others and illuminates the shape of their true identity. Showing up, staying awake, and being attentive in solitude shakes loose the hold of their addiction. By purposefully engaging solitude, Threes rediscover the truth that they don't need to prove their value to God before they pray and connect with the divine presence. Trusting that they are fully accepted and validated by God becomes the foundation to the restoration of their hope (page 211).

The Way Home for Four: *Rest in Solitude*

Intelligence Center	Heart/Feeling/Emotion
Harmony Triad	Idealist
Dominant Affect Group	Frustration
Prayer Posture	Solitude
Prayer Intention	Rest
Passion	Envy
Fixation	Melancholy
Holy Idea	Holy Origin
Virtue	Equanimity, Emotional Balance

The Challenge: Fours are drawn to deep feelings and often seem to drown in the intensity of their emotions. Due to the constant waves of emotions that they experience, they tend to fall asleep in the illusion that what they feel is more real than reality itself. Yet, their heart is a paradox; it can seem remarkably present to itself while simultaneously feeling cut off from itself, which fuels the lie that *they are what other people think or say about them.* The drive to find their identity and for others to affirm who they are can trap Fours in the chase to be seen.

The Invitation: By resting in solitude, Fours find the unexpected gift of being unseen which enables them to wake up and discover who they truly are. Many Fours feel isolated, but engaging solitude serves as a retreat from the strains and demands they experience. When Fours really allow themselves to rest, they receive the gift of their self-actualized, emotionally balanced, and wholly original essence. Turning down their anguish and breathing into their yearning to be known offers the soothing restoration only found in communion with God (page 214).

The Way Home for Five: *Consent to Silence*

Intelligence Center	Head/Mind/Thinking
Harmony Triad	Relationist
Dominant Affect Group	Rejection
Prayer Posture	Silence
Prayer Intention	Consent
Passion	Avarice
Fixation	Stinginess
Holy Idea	Holy Transparency
Virtue	Detachment

The Challenge: Though Fives are constantly analyzing information and can detect lies with lucidity, they still believe the lie that *they are what they have.* This illusion propels their compulsion toward mental activity and problem solving in order to possess answers. The incessant drive for data and solutions makes it challenging for Fives to detach from their own mental preoccupation and find contentment with who they are, and what they have, in the present moment.

The Invitation: Silence is necessary for Fives to turn down the exhausting mental obsession with finding answers. When they truly consent to silence, rather than attempting it for the sake of figuring out the fruit of contemplative practice, they are able to give themselves permission to detach from their own mental compulsion. Agreeing to silence means to make room in their minds to be present with God, and to permit divine interruptions and sacred answers to supersede their own cerebral efforts. Ultimately, they discover that they are accepted as they are and safe in the unknown (page 216).

The Way Home for Six: *Engage Silence*

Intelligence Center	Head/Mind/Thinking
Harmony Triad	Pragmatist
Dominant Affect Group	Attachment
Prayer Posture	Silence
Prayer Intention	Engage
Passion	Fear
Fixation	Cowardice
Holy Idea	Holy Strength, Faith
Virtue	Courage

The Challenge: Though in the middle of the Head Center, Sixes are disconnected from their rational mind and fall into anxiety-ridden threat forecasting. Fear is the life preserver that Sixes think will keep them from drowning, but, in reality, the worry it produces keeps them trapped. Sixes believe the lie that *they are what they have*, which fuels their compulsion to obtain security. Distracted, frenzied, and often weary from the burden of constantly looking for potential threats, Sixes find it difficult to give into the peace of the present moment or hear the voice of the Divine.

The Invitation: For Sixes to come home, they must reconnect with their Head Center and face their fears rationally. When they engage silence, their courage and strength emerge, and they are empowered to resist the illusion of their apprehensions. At first, silence seems as though it might amplify the fears of the Six, but by actively practicing silence they experience a cleansing from doubt, a cessation of worry, and a calming of their suspicions. When engaging silence with their whole self, Sixes can finally hear the truth of their resilient True Selves and open their faithful souls to the loving voice of God (page 128).

The Way Home for Seven: Rest in Silence

Intelligence Center	Head/Mind/Thinking
Harmony Triad	Idealist
Dominant Affect Group	Frustration
Prayer Posture	Silence
Prayer Intention	Rest
Passion	Gluttony
Fixation	Planning
Holy Idea	Holy Wisdom
Virtue	Sobriety

The Challenge: Without a direct connection to their hearts, Sevens fear and avoid their internal emotions like quicksand. They escape the pain, confusion, or complexity of their heart by filling life with every manner of fun they can think of. The constant search for the next fun thing and the joyful appreciation they receive from their social circles fuels the lie that *they are what they have*. The drive to have more—more people, places, things, and experiences—serves as a distracting feast from the disconnection inside but keeps them stuck swinging between the anticipation of the next thing and the frustration of never being satisfied.

The Invitation: Ironically for Sevens, true freedom is not found in chronic escapism but by resting in silence. Though slowing down and resting triggers the sinking feeling for Sevens, when they learn to truly rest in the quietness of their mind, they experience a liberation from their compulsive drive to plan the future and are able to embrace the present moment. When they consciously own their emotions, Sevens become refreshed by the rootedness of the now and reconnect with the wisdom that they already have everything they need to be truly content and completely loved by God (page 220).

The Way Home for Eight: *Consent to Stillness*

Intelligence Center	Body/Gut/Instinctive
Harmony Triad	Relationist
Dominant Affect Group	Rejection
Prayer Posture	Stillness
Prayer Intention	Consent
Passion	Lust
Fixation	Vengeance
Holy Idea	Holy Truth
Virtue	Innocence

The Challenge: As the type most connected to their bodies, Eights often use their physical presence to exert control or dominate their environments. Fueled by the lie that *they are what they do,* Eights are addicted to frenetic activity, which often leads them to overdoing everything. This compulsion often pushes them past their limits to exhaustion, and their aggressive, assertive social style can create discomfort or pain for others. It is extremely challenging for Eights to release control and trust their hidden vulnerabilities to God.

The Invitation: Consenting to stillness challenges the Eight to release control, a difficult task at first but one which enables them to find the peace and safety they long for. When making the deliberate choice to offer themselves to stillness, they might experience the discomfort of connecting to the Divine on God's terms and not theirs, but then discover the freedom and lightness of their own beloved innocence. When they let go and acknowledge that God is the only one in perfect control, they rest in the protection of the trustworthy presence of God (page 222).

The Way Home for Nine: *Engaging Stillness*

Intelligence Center	Body/Gut/Instinctive
Harmony Triad	Pragmatist
Dominant Affect Group	Attachment
Prayer Posture	Stillness
Prayer Intention	Engage
Passion	Sloth
Fixation	Indolence
Holy Idea	Holy Love
Virtue	Action

The Challenge: Those dominant in type Nine are most disconnected from their Body Center. When this disconnection is combined with the lie that *they are what they do*, Nines often fill the social role of mediator and reconciler, a skill at which they innately excel. However, this leads them to check out on life, seeking the interior calm they give to their external world. Tempted to fall asleep to themselves and to the life around them, Nines find it challenging to remain present in the moment and attuned to the presence of the Divine.

The Invitation: It is typically easy for Nines to be physically still, but actively engaging stillness requires that they show up and be intentionally present to themselves and the now. This practice activates the interior energies within Nines and reconnects them to their whole self—body, mind, and heart—thus enabling them to engage all the aspects of life that they neglect. This serves to meet the needs of true self-nurturing and self-protection that Nines seek but rarely find. When they attend stillness, Nines are refreshed by the active power of the love of God and are, in turn, energized to share this with their world.

"When we do the inner work required to wake up, to integrate the disconnected bits of ourselves, to dismantle the mythology of our ego projection, and to really tell ourselves the truth about who we are, then the growth we hope for sets in."

- We often choose to remain trapped in the cycle of our Passions and Fixations because we are convinced they serve us in some way, even though they are **unhealthy. What** do you receive from your Passions and Fixations?

_____

_____

_____

_____

_____

_____

- How would truly receiving your type's unique invitation as outlined above change **your internal thoughts and feelings?**

_____

_____

_____

_____

_____

_____

- What would your type's invitation mean for your relationship with friends and family?

_____

_____

_____

_____

_____

_____

- How would embracing your type's invitation change your relationship with God?

_____

_____

_____

_____

- The fruit of contemplative practice becomes evident after months of regular use. With what you know about yourself and your type, what challenges do you anticipate you'll face as you continue this journey?

_____

_____

_____

_____

_____

- What solutions, resources, or support do you need to create or recruit to ensure you have all that you need for lasting spiritual growth?

_____

_____

_____

_____

_____

DISCUSSION QUESTION

- Consider what practices, habits, or activities you gravitate toward when you feel the need to rest and recharge. How do these things provide or work against the solitude, silence, and stillness that you really need? Share with the group or reflect on how you might prioritize practices that cultivate more solitude, silence, and stillness in your life.

_____

_____

_____

_____

Invitation

Examen

The contemplative practice of Examen emerged from St. Ignatius of Loyola's *Spiritual Exercises* as a prayer to awaken consciousness to God's ever-present nearness. Through five reflective steps, Examen utilizes memory as a way to see how God moves toward us in very ordinary experiences throughout our day.

1. To begin, first recognize the presence of God with you, always present and always loving.

2. Move to reflective thanksgiving. Open your heart to gratitude and open your soul to be receptive to God.

3. Reflect on your day. Search the events, feelings, and thoughts you experienced for a moment in which you felt God moving toward or through you. This may be a small delight such as enjoying a cup of coffee in the morning or a sweet interaction with a loved one, or it may be a spark of grace such as receiving forgiveness, a profound conversation, or an encounter with God's reconciling presence.

4. In a similar manner to step three, search your day for a moment, attitude, thought, or experience in which you found yourself moving away from God's love and presence. Perhaps it was a moment when the voices in your head—fear, shame, distress, anger, guilt, disappointment, or regret—eclipsed the voice of Love. It's important to remember that it's not the person who hurt you that causes you to inch away from God but rather your resentful response toward that person; the family member who constantly annoys you isn't the cause for the regression but rather it is your impatience with them that causes you to suffer. Whatever form it took, acknowledge the experience with the gift of humble grace so that you are not overwhelmed by it.

5. With the thanksgiving and honesty of both moments, pray. Depending on the day, you may feel the need to express lament, repentance, sorrow, or an

appeal for help to let it go. Remember that God is bigger than your biggest problems, failures, hurts, and concerns.

6. Finally, close with hope for the future. Hold gratitude for past and future movements that will invite you to deeper growth. And rest in the hope of the coming gift of a new morning and new opportunities to connect with God.

—— Appendix ——

Growing in Your Contemplative Intention

To create a daily contemplative prayer practice of solitude, silence, and stillness, start by selecting one of the examples from any of the sessions' Invitation sections. Studies show those who spend about twenty minutes in contemplative prayer twice a day experience significant benefits after about six months. So, it is important to approach the practice with consistency and authenticity for some time to give contemplation a thorough try.

In the meantime, below are a few practical suggestions for finding moments of solitude, silence, and stillness in your day and to help ease you into contemplative practice.

BRINGING THE PRACTICE OF SOLITUDE INTO YOUR LIFE

- Set aside one day a week that you give yourself a break from social media and technology to help create a sense of detox from comparisons and the opinions of others.
- Make a habit of spending a few minutes alone every day doing something you enjoy just for yourself, not for how it helps your social status or for how it enables you to connect with others. Whether it's working on a pet project, going for a

quiet walk, or reading, this will help maintain your self-contentment and serve as a stepping-stone to the contemplative practice of solitude.

BUILDING THE PRACTICE OF SILENCE INTO YOUR LIFE

- Taking part in a physical activity that incorporates mental focus helps distract your mind from its incessant analyzing. Yoga, rock climbing, boxing, and mountain biking are just a few activities that direct your mind's focus to the task at hand and so, in a way, close the multiple browser tabs you have running in your brain. This is a helpful step in creating space for mental silence.
- Keep a running list of words, thoughts, impressions, or moments that you sense are from God. This may be a Scripture verse that touched you, something a friend said, or a thought that came to you in prayer. Writing them down in a journal will help train your thoughts to quiet down and prompt your mind to listen for the voice of Love.

GROWING THE PRACTICE OF STILLNESS

- Embrace and engage the moments of stillness throughout your day. When you find yourself waiting in traffic, for the coffee to brew, or to pick up your children from practice, resist the urge to create a to-do list, ruminate, or reach for your phone. Instead, take a few deep breathes, bring your mind to the present moment and give attention to your senses. What do you smell, hear, see? What do you notice happening in your body, heart, and mind? This mini practice will help ease the intensity of resistance to the present moment and bring you into deeper awareness of the beauty of the moment and your role in it.
- Train your mind to celebrate good things in your life such as friends, family, nature, and the small moments that brightened your day with beauty, belonging, laughter, and love. Regularly practicing gratitude for the little things brings balance and lightness to your thoughts and feelings. A helpful way to create this habit is by journaling "gratitude lists," or writing down one thing you're grateful for in your calendar at the end of each day.

THE BEGINNING OF A LIFELONG JOURNEY

Self-awareness is the beginning of liberation—and the Enneagram charts the way.

When we receive the personal insights revealed by the Enneagram, though some-times brutally honest, we can begin the inner work of dismantling our misperceptions about the world, ourselves, and God. We are then freed to integrate the disconnected bits of our identity and reconnect with our true essence. By aligning the holy giftings of our type, our Intelligence Centers, Harmony Triads, and Prayer Intentions, we finally awaken to the distinct way we were made to thrive.

Along the ever-progressing, always-deepening path into the contemplative postures of solitude, silence, and stillness, a new way of being opens—one of appreciation for your type's distinct qualities, attuning to the voice of Love, honoring the specific way each one of us experiences the Divine, and the sacred gift you bring to community. It's the way that will lead you home to the free, unique, and beloved person God created you to be.

Welcome to the journey home.

Resources

➤ To read more about Chris Heuertz and his work with the Enneagram and contemplative practice, visit www.chrisheuertz.com.

➤ For more contemplative practice tips and blogs, Enneagram workshops, personal coaching, and more, visit www.thegravitycenter.com.

➤ Singer and songwriter Ryan O'Neal, known publicly as *Sleeping at Last*, has composed and produced an album with beautiful songs about each Enneagram type, complete with special cover art. To listen and view, visit www.sleepingatlast.com/atlas. The *Sleeping at Last Podcast* offers great insights into the Enneagram and can be found everywhere podcasts are available.

➤ Both the Enneagram Institute and the EnneaApp are great places to explore the Enneagram and both offer respected tests.

Recommended Reading

Almaas, A. H. *Facets of Unity: The Enneagram of Holy Ideas*. Boston: Shambhala Publications, 1998.

Bakhtiar, Laleh. *The Sufi Enneagram: Sign of the Presence of God (Wajhullah): The Secrets of the Symbol Unveiled*. Chicago: Institute of Traditional Psychology, 2013.

Chestnut, Beatrice. *The Complete Enneagram: 27 Paths to Greater Self-Knowledge*. Berkeley, CA: She Writes Press, 2013.

Fernandez Christleib, Fatima. *Where (on Earth) Did the Enneagram Come From?* Ciudad de Mexico: Editorial Pax Mexico, 2016.

Ichazo, Óscar. *Between Metaphysics and Protoanalysis: A Theory for Analyzing the Human Psyche*. New York: Arica Institute Press, 1982.

Maitri, Sandra. Foreword to *The Enneagram of Passions and Virtues: Finding the Way Home* by A. H. Almaas. New York: Penguin, 2005.

———. *The Spiritual Dimension of the Enneagram: The Nine Faces of the Soul*. New York: TarcherPerigee, 2001.

Naranjo, Claudio. *Character and Neurosis: An Integrative View*. Nevada City, NV: Gateways/IDHHB Publishers, 1994.

Palmer, Helen. *The Enneagram in Love and Work: Understanding Your Business and Intimate Relationships*. New York: HarperOne, 1995.

———. *The Enneagram: Understanding Yourself and the Others in Your Life*. New York: HarperOne, 1998.

Riso, Don Richard, and Russ Hudson. *The Wisdom of the Enneagram: The Complete Guide to Psychological and Spiritual Growth for the Nine Personality Types*. New York: Bantam, 1999.

Rohr, Richard, and Andreas Ebert. *The Enneagram: A Christian Perspective*. Translated by Peter Heinegg. New York: Crossroad, 2006.

The Sacred Enneagram

Finding Your Unique Path to Spiritual Growth

Christopher L. Heuertz

A must-read for anyone looking to move beyond type as caricature and learn how to work with the Enneagram toward spiritual growth. Over 100,000 copies sold!

Most of us spend a lifetime trying to figure out who we are, and how we relate to others and God. The Enneagram is here to help. Far more than a personality test, author Chris Heuertz writes, the Enneagram is a sacred map to the soul. Lies about who we think we are keep us trapped in loops of self-defeat. But the Enneagram reveals both the nine ways we get lost, as well as the nine ways we find our way home to our True Self and to God.

Chris Heuertz has taught the Enneagram all over the world, and has trained under some of the great living Enneagram masters including Father Richard Rohr, Russ Hudson, Marion Gilbert, and Helen Palmer. Whether you are an enthusiast or simply Enneagram-curious, this groundbreaking guide to the spiritual depth of the Enneagram will help you:

- Understand the "why" behind your type, beyond caricatures and stereotypes
- Identify and find freedom from self-destructive patterns
- Learn how to work with your type toward spiritual growth
- Awaken your unique gifts to serve today's broken world

Richly insightful and deeply practical, *The Sacred Enneagram* is your invitation to begin the journey of a life transformed.

Available in stores and online!